Greater Than a Tourist
Kolkata
West Bengal
India

50 Travel Tips from a Local

Anisha Mandal

Copyright © 2017 CZYK Publishing
All Rights Reserved. No part of this publication may be reproduced, including scanning and photocopying, or distributed in any form or by any means, electronic or mechanical, or stored in a database or retrieval system without prior written permission from the publisher.

Disclaimer: The publisher has put forth an effort in preparing and arranging this book. The information provided herein by the author is provided "as is". Use this information at your own risk. Consult your doctor before engaging in any medical activities. The publisher and author disclaim any liabilities for any loss of profit or commercial or personal damages resulting from the information contained in this book.

Order Information: To order this title please email lbrenenc@gmail.com or visit GreaterThanATourist.com. A bulk discount can be provided.

Cover Template Creator: Lisa Rusczyk Ed. D. using Canva.
Cover Creator: Lisa Rusczyk Ed. D.
Image: https://pixabay.com/en/victoria-memorial-india-kolkata-2394784/

Lock Haven, PA
All rights reserved.
ISBN: 9781549882043

>TOURIST

Anisha Mandal

BOOK DESCRIPTION

Are you excited about planning your next trip?

Do you want to try something new?

Would you like some guidance from a local?

If you answered yes to any of these questions, then this Greater Than a Tourist book is for you.

Greater Than a Tourist- Kolkata, India by Anisha Mandal offers the inside scoop on Kolkata. Most travel books tell you how to sightsee. Although there's nothing wrong with that, as a part of the Greater than a Tourist series, this book will give you tips from someone who lives at your next travel destination. In these pages, you'll discover local advice that will help you throughout your trip.

Travel like a local. Slow down and get to know the people and the culture of a place. By the time you finish this book, you will be eager and prepared to travel to your next destination.

Anisha Mandal

TABLE OF CONTENTS

BOOK DESCRIPTION

TABLE OF CONTENTS

DEDICATION

ABOUT THE AUTHOR

FROM THE PUBLISHER

WELCOME TO > TOURIST

INTRODUCTION

1. Your Quintessential Bangali

2. Getting Around the City- Spoiled for Choice

3. The Gastronomical Art of Street Food

4. The Lanes of Nostalgia- North Kolkata

5. The 'Para' or Neighbourhood Culture

6. The Calendar of Festivals

7. A Book Lover's Dreams Translated

8. The Stage is Always Set

9. Rock is a Lifestyle

10. Cricket is a Lifestyle

11. Football is a Never ending Courtship

12. Sudder Street- Your Indispensable Bohemian Rhapsody

13. After China's own heart- India's only Chinatown

14. Nahoum and Sons- Our Jewish Willy Wonka Clan

15. Incomplete without Tea

16. All about Sweet Nothings

17. The Immortality of Rabindranath Tagore

18. City of Antiquities

19. Your Coyness, Victoria Memorial

20. A Day in the Museum

21. Forever Young at 250: The Great Banyan Tree

22. A Novice's Guide to Shopping for the Right Saree

23. Dhoti Secrets: The Fashionista in the Bengali Man

24. The Ghats- A City Outlined by the Ganges

25. We're a Fishy Lot

26. As Grave as it Gets

27. India's First Organ Sits Shy Here: St. John's Cathedral

28. Vociferous Debating- Ends with Songs and Hugs

29. Night Crawlers, Ahoy!

30. The Race Course- Just like Old Times!

31. The Wedding Reds, Whites and Golds

32. The Political Artery

33. Biryani. Period.

34. A Filmlover's Muse

35. The Inviting Campus Culture- Jadavpur University

36. Checkmate Under a Flyover

37. The Infectious Energy of Local Markets

38. New Market- Some Things Never Go Out of Vogue

39. A Clayman's Breathing Ground

40. Suruchi Restaurant- By women who don't need justification since 1969

41. 130 Year Old Flower Market

42. You're Never Too Old for Music- Instruments from Bengal

43. Birla Mandir- Years of Hardwork

44. Nakhoda Masjid- Leftovers of Akbar's Influence

45. Romancing by the Lake

46. Saltlake, Rajarhat: Kolkata Spreads Wings

47. The Tramconductor's Ting-ting-ting

48. Oil Lamps and Chanting by the Ganges- Belur Math

49. Marble Palace- 19th Century Elegance

Anisha Mandal

50. The Kolkata Soundscape

Top Reasons to Book This Trip

Our Story

Notes

DEDICATION

To Nia, a name in gibberish that I lovingly call my grandmother by, which happened to catch on in my social circles effortlessly. Her countless anecdotes brought me up and grew her old. A quilt through all the thunderstorms that came by me, she is a summary of all that is bitter-sweet in my endless love affair with Kolkata. To my grandfather, who back in 1998 told me how small the world really is. Under his guidance, my fingers learned to run gleefully through the index of Reader's Digest's World Atlas, the age-old 1961 edition. A decade later, I learned to love backpacks.

Anisha Mandal

ABOUT THE AUTHOR

Anisha Mandal is a full-time dreamer. When she's not dreaming, she is working on a craft to translate it into reality. The 23-year-old visual storyteller, writer and theatre artist has spent the majority of her life in Kolkata, before shifting base to Mumbai, the next most romantic metropolitan city in India, to explore the art of filmmaking.

Her nomadic heart will always stay stuck on age-old Indian film songs and will often whisper lines from the poems of the great Faiz Ahmed Faiz, Mirza Ghalib, and Agha Shahid Ali. Her nimble feet dance at the thought of creating unforgettable stories and memories with people from across the world. Of course, over great food, just the way they'd cook it in their own kitchens.

Anisha Mandal

HOW TO USE THIS BOOK

The Greater Than a Tourist book series was written by someone who has lived in an area for over three months. The goal of this book is to help travelers either dream or experience different locations by providing opinions from a local. The author has made suggestions based on their own experiences. Please do your own research before traveling to the area in case the suggested places are unavailable.

Anisha Mandal

FROM THE PUBLISHER

Traveling can be one of the most important parts of a person's life. The anticipation and memories that you have are some of the best. As a publisher of the Greater Than a Tourist book series, as well as the popular 50 Things to Know book series, we strive to help you learn about new places, spark your imagination, and inspire you. Wherever you are and whatever you do I wish you safe, fun, and inspiring travel.

Lisa Rusczyk Ed. D.

CZYK Publishing

Anisha Mandal

WELCOME TO > TOURIST

Anisha Mandal

INTRODUCTION

2nd October 2017 | 7:00 a.m

Dear Reader,

I have spent the last two weeks on a couch in Mumbai writing to you, as my entire city was busy celebrating one of the biggest festivals known to India and the world- Durga Pujo. You see for us, Pujo is less religious and more soul-matter. You really must be special. I want you to know that the next hundreds odd pages are full of my fondest memories in and of a city that will forever be my first romance; that every person who has ever lived in my little battleground of dreams feels the same way about it. You are about to read and hopefully, someday visit a city where romance is not a flavor of playful flirtations, but the kind that you talk to your grandchildren about in top-secrecy. You are about to read my memories of an unforgettably poignant childhood and dynamic, zestful coming of age. I have handpicked the most precious facets of Kolkata for you and hope that you would have had a collection of immeasurable stories in your suitcases on your journey back from my city. Of course, for the fear of all the pages of the world expiring if I were to write all that I want to tell you, I have knowingly missed out on a few aspects; I understand that your trip may not be very long, while I also thrill myself with the imagination that there are a few things that you had better figure out on your own. I'd like to lead you to the magic, not perform it for you. My city does not come close to featuring on the top travel portals of the world- it's not a Paris, it's not a London, or a Tokyo, or a Beijing, or a New York. It's not lavish, nor does it possess vast landscapes of grandeur. It is exquisite but heck, so is all of Europe or the oriental islands. But I can promise you that a Kolkata is an emotional journey like no other; like the last cup of coffee with the protagonist of your unrequited love story. So, as we Bangalis whisper, to wish someone luck before a journey-

"Dugga Dugga!"

1. Your Quintessential Bangali

An eternal love for great food, an undying thirst to master an art form, tremendous grit to keep learning about the workings of the world, perpetual eagerness to stay updated on the latest news, a distinct understanding of the political landscape of the country and the world with significant opinions about most socio-economic factors, boasting both the history of imperialism and the indispensable role they played in India's Nationalist Struggle against the British Raj, proud of its array of accomplished poets, writers, painters, dancers, scientists, teachers, doctors, engineers, lawyers who chase their dreams like a lover pursuing that one great romance carrying the heart at the edge of a flimsy sleeve, your quintessential Bangali or Bengali is an ethnic group originating from the region of Bengal in South Asia.

A trip to Kolkata, the capital of West Bengal and (rightfully) hailed as the cultural capital of India, is worthwhile just to mingle with the Bengali kin, though you can safely be taken by surprise if you're not already at a social distance of a single degree of separation from a Bengali already - we are all over the world and very social by nature. There's always a slight conflict of discourse in terms of the name of this vibrant city; the average Bengali is torn between calling it Calcutta, a name handed over by the British during their woefully long 200-year-old regime in India, and Kolkata, as the city is called in Bangla, the mother tongue of the Bengalis. While Calcutta reeks of nostalgia which comes as easily to Calcuttans as tomatoes to Spain, Kolkata spells relevance, passion, and pride, distinctly visible in the intonations with which it is pronounced in conversation.

You can pick either and be rest assured that the streets will be bustling with overtly helpful people who will gleefully take it upon themselves to help you with directions and suggestions at all hours of the day. "Calcutta's the only city I know where you are actively encouraged to stop strangers at random for a quick chat." – Tahir Shah, Sorcerer's Apprentice.

Interestingly, Kolkata is one of the most cosmopolitan cities of the country and the gigantic spectrum of people from different communities that you meet will always place their Kolkata connect right on top of the various other factors that comprise their identity. Keep a keen ear for all the cutesy subtexts that lace their gestures, take a whiff of why they are all such a spirited lot and you will be left with a broad grin as you realise that the people of Kolkata are not just inherently in love with its diversity - they find the oddest of reasons, every passing day, to celebrate it, even if it's solely in their regular passionate style of conversation.

2. Getting Around the City- Spoiled for Choice

I cannot help but recount what the memorable character Hasari Pal says in Roland Joffe's 1992 film City of Joy (which is what Kolkata is most commonly called). He poignantly states, "If the journey is not what you expected, do not be surprised."

The hand-pulled two (daringly, three sometimes) seater rickshaw, the cycle rickshaw, the four (daringly, five when the cops aren't looking) seater auto-rickshaw, the State transport not-so-mini Mini buses, the newly introduced A.C buses, the yellow Ambassador taxis, the new-age No Refusal cabs, the underground Metro, the thriving Uber and Ola business, the efficient local train system, the Ferry and Launch services, the wooden boats and fully-functional trams that I vividly discuss in the coming chapters and the joy of walking through the streets painted in all sorts of vintage meets post modern art shades, getting around in the city is fairly easy and unimaginably inexpensive. I remember covering a distance of 8 kms in 8 odd Indian rupees. Using the public transport will benefit your Kolkata experience immensely. The slow, rhythmic tempo of the city interlaced with the distinct, exclusive humdrum is best felt during these teensy journeys to and from a place. For all you know, you will end up discovering a corner that not even people from the city knew existed.

Go with your instincts, know that you're safe, wear the heart of an adventure-loving bohemian and you're good to go.

3. The Gastronomical Art of Street Food

At this point, there are a couple of statements that I must make and you must believe like it's straight out of your most important religious text.

You cannot be in Kolkata and not love to eat. You must be a sport and reduce your hygiene standards (there are one too many medical shops to offer you antacids, often strategically located right beside restaurants). You need to plan your food wisely and safe enough room at all times for you never know what exquisite delicacy you might chance upon.

Here are names of must-try you might want to make a note of- Phuchka, Chicken/Mutton Roll, Dahi- Papri- Chaat, Ghoti-Garam, Chicken Chowmein and Chilly Chicken (Indo-Chinese is a legitimate cuisine that is Kolkata's expertise). Make sure you chance upon a tea-stall and ask for a Double-Egg Omlette with Bread or Bread-Ghoogni (Chickpea curry is the closest I could come to translating it right). Wash it all down with Sugarcane Juice or Coconut Water. Take my word for it. The joy that you will receive despite the possibility of a little dose of tummy-rumbles is more than just worth it.

4. The Lanes of Nostalgia- North Kolkata

North Kolkata, even by the generally old-school standards of Kolkata as a whole, is a fascinating part of Kolkata that is situated in the timeline of the past, almost as if someone froze time and moments there in the 80s and there was no desire of awakening from the spell. Tiny lanes, weaved together, through buildings that are easily a century old. Laid-back is a trait that you can almost take for granted here. But, the body language of the people and the aura of the moss-stained walls guarding the unique intricacies of the marvels of architecture should not give you the impression of this part of the city being any less loud and boisterous than the rest of it. In fact, it often is the happiest kind of rowdy that you've ever come across. All sorts of businesses thrive here. Lines of shops for wedding cards, paper, grains, kites, spices, there's nothing that you won't find in North Kolkata. If you'd like an authentic feel of

Kolkata, this is where you'll have to be. The most amount of clinging on to tradition is right here. Interestingly, North Kolkata is also home to Asia's largest red-light district, which is definitely a commentary on the fabric of society across time brackets. Here are the names of a few lanes that you might want to recall during your visit around this place:

Shovabazaar, Shyambazaar, Manicktala, Belgachhia, Chitpur, Bagbazaar, the incredibly famous College Street which carries a part of every Bengali's heart and the renowned Sealdah Station.

5. The 'Para' or Neighbourhood Culture

A very critical part of friendships and social relationships in Kolkata is the beautiful 'Para' or culture of the neighbourhood. This geo-emotional sentiment is deeply infused with a feeling of togetherness and belonging particular to the street or locality where one lives. Women and men of the same neighbourhood make and break relationships with each other all the time over simple occasions and pettiness respectively. However, if trouble casts a shadow on the locality, not a spare thought is invested before standing up for each other. Shopping for food and clothes together, discussing domestic issues across subjects ranging from frivolous scandals to parental worries and detailed discussions about food and weather, always stopping by each other on the common street to passionately discuss the latest fads, celebrity gossips, the socio-economic framework of the country and India's performance in a sport, the members of every Para celebrate all the major festivals together.

The celebrated Bengali actor-director-writer-musician, Anjan Dutta, opens one of his playful romantic numbers with the words- "Para-e dhukle thyang khora kore debo, boleche Para'r Dada Ra. Onno para diye jachhi tayi", which literally translates into- "The elder-brothers of the neighbourhood have warned me that if I walk into this locality, my legs will be broken. Hence, I am going to go through a different locality." This should paint an image of a locality which lives more like a family. Each member of a locality, irrespective of the different families that they hail from, have a certain role and are called by a certain title. These titles are also used in familial relationships, thus verifying how every Para is one gigantic unit on its own. I am enlisting a few of these Titles, roles and the characteristics of the people bearing them, since a trip to Kolkata will invariably ascertain your hearing them more often than not.

Dada or Elder Brother- Pronounced with a soft D, every man who looks like he is in the age group of 25 to 35 years, can safely be called Dada. There are extremely amiable Dadas who will help you get by in Kolkata. There are also very dominating Dadas who'd like to believe that they have just walked out of some extremely badass gangster movie. They love being the one-stop solution to all your woes. Interestingly, one of the most celebrated Indian cricketers of all time, Sourav Ganguly is lovingly called Dada.

Didi or Elder Sister is the female counterpart of the Dada. Interestingly, Mamata Banerjee, the current Chief Minister of West Bengal is most popularly called Didi by one and all, irrespective of where one's political allegiance lies.

Kaka/Kaku or Uncle, Father's younger-brother to be precise, is an older version of Dada and would be believed to have more wisdom on him. The Kaku is your go-to person. Call your average shopkeeper Kaku, watch him melt a little and have your work done faster, perhaps with more insight.

Kakima is the female counterpart of Kaku. Of what I have mostly seen, Kakimas are always dollops of joy.

Dadu or Grandfather, pronounced with a soft D, is the most sought-after man in the Para. With all the information in the world about any given subject and an incredible sense of humour, this man will speak to you like he was the protagonist of Jules Verne's Around the World in 80 days. If you catch him in a good mood, he might sing a few lines from his favourite songs for you. If he's not particularly happy, he will criticise everything under the sun. Either way, this story teller has a lot of blessings to bestow upon you.

Dida or Grandmother is the female counterpart of the Dadu and the only person the Dadu might just cower in front of. Her culinary skills make all the Michelin stars of the world disappear into a distant horizon and if you appear too thin, by her standards, she will immediately get concerned and take up the mission of restoring your health by adding generous bouts of butter to your meals. She will always have a beauty tip for you and her knowledge about fabrics is unparalleled. Her tips about being penny wise could put a lot of the world's best financial advisors to shame. You can safely swear by her sense of aesthetics and taste in music.

I could go on forever, but I must leave something to your discoveries too. I will, thus, rest it here.

6. The Calendar of Festivals

"Baro maash e tero parbon" or Thirteen Festivals in Twelve Months, is a very commonly used playful Bangla phraseology which is a commentary on how life in West Bengal is centred around celebrations. With an array of festivals inherent to the gamut of religions and communities who call the land home, at any given month of the year, you are bound to be a part of some celebration of sorts.

There are essentially two kinds of festivals in India- the first kind are the ones that are timed in accordance to the regional or religious calendars which are mostly lunar calendars and abide by the five seasons of the country (according to the Bangla calendar, 2017 is 1424- reading up about how it is calculated might be interesting for you); the second kind of festivities follow the Gregorian calendar and typically celebrate a National hero's life event.

What is however, interesting for Bengalis is that a day-off for celebration is scarcely ever a single day off. There's almost always an extra day that the Bengali chromosome requires to return to the monotony of daily life. While some perceive it as the work of the lazy bone, for us it is simply looking at every day as a tiny part of a life well lived.

Eid, Muharram, Navroz, Saraswati Puja, Durga Puja, Poila Baisakh (our New Year), Rabindra Jayanti, Ratha Jatra, Holi or Dol Puja are some of the festivals that you might want to plan your trip around.

7. A Book Lover's Dreams Translated

Mildly putting it, Kolkata is home to the second largest book hub of the world and the largest in India. Two words- College Street. An expanse of North Kolkata dedicated to a myriad book shops, a lot of which dedicate themselves to memorialize second hand books across genres and eras and tastes, always open to bargaining almost like a year round sale- that's what dreams are made up of. A conversation with the shopkeepers broadens your worldview like no other. The reading habit is more often than not aggressively encouraged in the average Bengali household and tends to cling onto those subjected to it as a lifestyle intricacy that makes sure that of all the transitory things in vogue in the world, books always remain as a priority on the list of investments a Bengali makes in their lifetimes. So the next time you find the average Bangali quoting a line from their favourite verse you don't have to be in awe or surprise- one of the few times I undauntedly generalise. There are countless street corners across the city that cater to the bookworms in Kolkata, some of which are situated in Golpark in South Kolkata and Park Street.

There's also the Oxford Bookstore, now equipped to serve you coffee as you read a book before picking it up. It's timeless and exclusive, hence finding a loyalist in me.

8. The Stage is Always Set

A rich, proud history in the performing arts always bestows responsibility to carry on with the tradition and Kolkata works towards upholding its theatre legacy while evolving everyday to embrace the emerging waves in the art form. Nandan is called the theatre-locality of Kolkata where performances by various renowned and emerging groups happen every day. The many government halls are almost always packed, mostly with dates that are taken a year in advance. The modern theatre performance spaces like Gyan Manch, G.D Birla Sabhaghar and Kala Mandir find themselves with packed weeks all year round. The young theatre groups which specialize in presenting multilingual, mixed art spectacles unfailingly surprise the theatre-goers. Of course, theatre is often recognised in the region as a not-very profitable branch of the show business, but passion rules the romance with the stage. Here are some auditoriums with schedules that you might want to keep a look out for:

Academy of Fine Arts, the open air space at Nandan, Madhusudan Manch, G.D Birla Sabhaghar, Gyan Manch, Kala Mandir, Kala Kunj, Vidya Mandir, among others.

Don't forget to pay a visit to Star Theatre, built in 1883. Back in the day, when the red carpet would roll at the Star Theatre, evenings celebrated theatre artists with the fervour that is similar to that at any International Award Ceremonies.

9. Rock is a Lifestyle

Let's put it mildly and simply throw a fact your way- West Bengal's first rock band was also India's first rock band. With a variety of influences from all around the world, Moheener Ghoraguli was formed when the world was observing the Vietnam War and the Naxal movement, sometime in 1975. Kolkata's rock scene has only surged ahead since then and the love for the genre only paved ways for other genres to find nativity in the city. There are numerous Bangla phrases which are indicative of the fact that since the 1980s, regular households have purchased musical instruments like never before. Of course, the tradition of the folk baul music and the huge influence that Rabindra-Sangeet (songs written and composed by Rabindranath Tagore, a tradition that is widely sworn by) always made the average Bangali adept to having a natural inclination towards music as an art form, but the coming-of-age rock-period of Kolkata made sure that the young Bangali girl or boy, could now express their coming-of-age woes by making their little heart breaks and aspirations privy to the songs they were listening to and singing out. There's a reason why a particular discipline taught at a particular University in Kolkata has Bob Dylan and The Beatles as significant parts of the syllabus. With commercial rock bands emerging in almost every other street, there had to be emerging platforms where the bands would end up performing. Currently, numerous pubs, restaurants, stages host musicians on a regular basis. You cannot go to Kolkata and not pay a visit to Someplace Else at The Park Hotel situated in Park Street. It is one of the oldest stages for musicians and lovers of live performances to unwind together.

If you're lucky, you'll find yourself at a street corner where a couple of boys have decided to do their version of a buskers act. You might also want to be in sync with a few Bangla artists. I'm listing my favourite ones here-

Moheener Ghoraguli, Chandrabindoo, Fossils, Bhoomi, Anjan

Dutta, Pinknoise. A few of my personal favourite young, emerging bands would be- What Escapes Me, Chronic Xorn, Gingerfeet, Underground Authority, The Ganesh Talkies, The High Crook, Neel and the Lightbulbs, Preying Mantis, The Radical Array Project.

10. Cricket is a Lifestyle

Yes, the British brought it with them. But we have our ways in making things our own. It is a fact well known that India is a land that is home to many a religion and belief. Then there is cricket. A household religion for all. Kolkata is home to the India's largest cricket stadium- The Eden Gardens. That itself must say a lot about how important cricket is to Kolkata. The Indian Cricket Team for Men's Cricket which is one of the most applauded sporting teams of the world across different sports was fortunate to call this particular, extremely admirable cricketer its captain- Sourav Ganguly, who is often called The Royal Bengal Tiger for his fierce grace on and off the field. Watching a cricket match at The Eden Gardens is an experience you must allow yourself to have. If not, there are cricket academies all across the city, in every possible locality- just grab an early morning slot to watch the little-big aspiring cricketers enjoying a good game, or simply spend an evening in a locality- wait till the bats, wickets and balls come out of the house to enjoy a good game, unfailingly.

"Alice sighed wearily. 'I think you might do something better with the time,' she said, 'than waste it in asking riddles that have no answers.'

'If you knew Time as well as I do,' said the Hatter, 'you wouldn't talk about wasting it. It's him.'

'I don't know what you mean,' said Alice.

'Of course you don't!' the Hatter said, tossing his head contemptuously. 'I dare say you never even spoke to Time!'

'Perhaps not,' Alice cautiously replied: 'but I know I have to beat time when I learn music.'

`Ah! that accounts for it,' said the Hatter. `He won't stand beating. Now, if you only kept on good terms with him, he'd do almost anything you liked with the clock. For instance, suppose it were nine o'clock in the morning, just time to begin lessons: you'd only have to whisper a hint to Time, and round goes the clock in a twinkling! Half-past one, time for dinner!"

- Lewis Carroll

Anisha Mandal

11. Football is a Never ending Courtship

If you have a vague idea of what Madrid and Barcelona might be like during El Clasico or North London during the Derby, you will get the idea of the air in Kolkata during the East Bengal-Mohun Bagan matches. Fiercely in love with the sport, following every possible game across the world religiously, playing it in every odd public park- with or without the right shoes, in every odd weather, cussing international players for that one wrong move, making a conversation worth an entire evening to applaud that great goal or that great save, across age groups, occupations, football has united and divided Bengal in so many ways than one. Catch a great game or slip in football in a conversation, the Bangali will love you ever more for the passion that you show for something that tugs at all the right chords of the aching, football loving heart.

12. Sudder Street- Your Indispensable Bohemian Rhapsody

Hash and hippies was a legitimate Kolkata thing since the 70s and though very understated now, Kolkata pretty much boasts the culture in all its artistic glory and the fashion that it brings with it. If one was to go on a Hippie trail, they were sure to land themselves in Sudder Street at some point or the other. Rows of hotels lined for tourists from across the world looking forward to a very cheap stay, rows of restaurants and pubs, located right beside Kolkata's oldest shopping complex on one of Kolkata's oldest roads, bordered by curio shops, visited frequently by roadside hawkers selling musical instruments and handmade-homemade perfumes, this place is fascinating as it observes all the cultures in the world bump into each other and paint a low-lit canvas with kaleidoscopic colours. It is indeed, a must visit or a must-stay locality, however you'd prefer it.

13. After China's own heart- India's only Chinatown

Mahjong clubs, a Chinese printing press, excellent shoe makers, awe-inspiring hairstylists, one of the most vibrant Chinese New Years, a large expanse full of family-run Chinese restaurants- Kolkata's Chinatown will lend you the flavor of China in the heart of the city while also shedding light on how fascinated the rest of the country is with the culture and cuisine of the clan who settled in India. A meal for two at INR 700 leaving you craving for more with no tummy-room to spare, Kim Ling is the restaurant I swear by.

The once-opium den Tirreti Bazaar that offers the world-famous Chinese breakfast at 6.30 a.m is not as great as it used to be, but still worth a visit, just for the experience.

If your trip coincides with the Chinese New Year celebrations, you are in for the best dumpling treat of your life. The Indian Chinese have a way with the way they celebrate and in general, are. Dragon and Lion dances while you wait to pick up that customized, inexpensive, dream pair of shoes made for you specially by great craftsmen, and authentic Chinese newspapers, with lovely, old Chinese women whose golden teeth shine of history- this is a priority visit.

14. Nahoum and Sons- Our Jewish Willy Wonka Clan

By now, you must have a fair idea of how Kolkata is a land of settlers from all sorts of places in the world and are more than just delighted to embrace what they brought and made, with loyal gratitude. Taking you back in time, this extremely famous but very understated bakery situated in New Market is going to leave you clueless about what not to gorge on. That rich fruit cake, that lemon tart, those cheese-everythings, how inexpensive all of it is- sometimes I legitimately miss Kolkata just because of places like Nahoum's. Our yuletide season has always meant quite a little Nahoum-time and we take our Yuletide season, very, very seriously. A very special kind of winter in Kolkata is never done right without a rum ball from Nahoum's, or two, or three, or… Where are my tickets to Kolkata already!

15. Incomplete without Tea

I will try to put this as simply as the fact that we, are, essentially, almost, all of us, positively, addicted, to tea. We call it Cha, pronounced just like that- like cha-cha-cha. Our culture is tea-centric. Our conversations or 'adda' as we call it, are over tea. We can legitimately consuming an easy 5-6 cups of tea every day. We fancy not-very-healthy biscuits with tea. Every street corner has a roadside tea-stall. Our tea is all milk and sugar. Our tea-stalls start their day's business as early as 4 a.m. Our tea-stalls are equipped to serve bread and egg. Our tea-stalls also have sweets that we like to consume with our tea (my favourite being this deep fried sweet called Goja). Our tea-stalls has brewed the most intellectual ideas of all time. Our tea-stalls have seen relationships being made and broken. Our tea-stalls have seen political decisions being made and debated. Our tea-stalls always offer cigarettes and Bengal consumes a lot of cigarettes(the Bengal beedi is a tiny thin cigarette which is made up of tobacco rolled in dried betel leaves and tied together with a string), because the average tea and all the heavy-duty culture that surrounds it triggers the need for nicotine for the average Bangali who has been trying to quit for years, in vain.

We are also awfully close to Darjeeling which makes the tea-connoisseurs keep an addicted eye on the first flush or second flush or the oolongs and whatever other tea they can lay their hands on. Milk, sugar, no milk with sugar, no sugar no milk, with cardamoms, with cloves, without any spices, with vanilla, or cinnamon, or simply unhealthy- acidity inducing stale leaf tea, from Assam or Darjeeling or other places in the world- We love our tea.

Does not make us not love coffee. But, oh well.

16. All about Sweet Nothings

Mishti which translates into the word Sweet is an emotion- it is an adjective for lovely people, it is an adjective for something or someone pretty, it is what the Bengali language is hailed as, and it is an unimaginably vast variety of desserts, except that Bangalis can dessert all the time in their lives. A sweet shop or Mishti'r Dokaan is as commonly found as the tea-stalls, and I have scarcely chanced upon a sweet shop that is below average in what they make. I happen to have 28 sweet-teeth placed carefully on my jaws that exist only for these delicacies, zero exaggeration. The Roshogolla is an art form in itself. Chhena or unrefined cheese rolled out in heavenly round balls with sugar syrup to create this magic is something I'd like to eat for my last meal on this planet. And at least four of them in one go. I am going to enlist a few names of sweets that you absolutely MUST try, when in Kolkata and the names of a few of my favourite sweet shops. If you can't pronounce it, take a picture of this page and point it out to people in Kolkata, they'll be more than glad to help you out. While you're at it, eat some on my behalf and if you feel like thanking me in life for the same, which is an inevitable possibility, write to the publisher enquiring about my address and let me know. I'll send recipes across.

Sweets (to die for):

Pantua, Chhana'r Jilipi, Kheer'er Chop, Taal Shnaash Bhora Shondesh, Chom Chom. Roshomalayi, Rabri, Indrani, Dilkhush, Shor Bhaja.

My favourite sweet shops:

Banchharam and Sons, Balaram Mullick and Radharam Mullick, Ganguraam and Sons, K.C Das and Sons, Mouchak, Girish Chandra Dey, Putiram.

Owing to a rapid transformation and modernisation, most of these sweet shops now have websites that you can look up for you to pre-order sweets. However, don't shy away from stopping by just about ANY sweet shop and trying whatever looks great to your eye. The shopkeeper or Mishtiwala will be thrilled to put in his recommendations.

17. The Immortality of Rabindranath Tagore

"Nayano tomarey paaye na dekhite, royecho nayan e nayan e"
These eyes don't get to catch sight of you. You, however, remain as a sight in my eyes.

Philsopher, poet, lyricist, music composer, playwright, painter, essayist, seeker of spirituality, seer, educationist, academician, rebel, crucial part of the Nationalist struggle against British imperialism, visionary and Nobel laureate- The heart of Bengal rightfully belongs to Rabindranath Tagore. His date of birth is a day of celebration for Bangalis across the world, a calendar holiday in West Bengal. His death anniversary is a day when our eyes well up inadvertently. Our traffic signals blare his songs. Our children learn to dance with his songs. There's barely a thought or philosophy that this man here hasn't written about. I'm honestly petrified of penning down this chapter for the knowledge that the greatest writers and philosophers across the world have written unending pages of literature about this man and still feel inadequate.

A trip to Kolkata is incomplete without paying a visit to Jorasanko Thakur Bari, his ancestral home. Hailing from the most respected family in all of Bengal, a visit Dwarkanath Tagore Lane is exhilarating.

Pick up a copy of Tagore, purchase a cassette or two, read a few odd poems, bask in the overwhelming emotion that Gitanjali is- you will have learned more about life than most of your life's experiences put together.

18. City of Antiquities

I swear it with my heart crossed- just walking around in Kolkata will make you stumble upon little pieces of history; in pebbles, in little street side stores which frame pictures, with hawkers thinking of how to sell an experience with their little array of collectibles, in coins, in stamps, in clothes, every odd where. Curio shopping is easiest done in a place with timelines that cling on to fond memories of the past.

The curio shops in Kolkata are in abundance. Particularly notable are the ones situated in Park Street. I remember picking up this Navy Cut tin container, the first of its kind to come into India for a dear friend, and I swear I could have packed up the whole of that shop or better still made a home out of it, immediately. The Auction House in Kolkata on Sundays is another unforgettable experience. The oldest clocks, the most beautiful mirrors, other instruments of interest, things reeking of rich histories, being auctioned off, often in the presence of their owners who give them away with heavy hearts. The rest of your curio shopping can all happen in New Market. Gorgeous jewellery, scarves, other tiny artefacts, name it and there it is. And pretty inexpensive at that.

19. Your Coyness, Victoria Memorial

Of all the marble wonders of the world, my partial heart has found the most amount of solace in the company of the hundreds of house martins that are silent playful children in the Victoria Memorial's premises. Understated and gorgeous- just the way I like my monuments best, the Victoria Memorial was conceptualized by George Curzon to embody the Indo-Saracenic revivalistic style. The angel that sits right on top of the Victoria Memorial, once upon a time, would spin, they say.

Recent renovations have installed lights in the premises but it is a sight to behold as it is. It's location makes it all the more gorgeous. Right opposite the famous Maidan, a huge expanse of green, with horses trotting by all the time, tonga rides available for tourists (that I don't advocate because it's plain animal torture), and an uncanny feeling of stillness, the Victoria Memorial is a visit that should ideally occupy the whole of the first half of the day.

Home to 25 odd galleries, the light and sound show which is held every day except Mondays and National Holidays is quite a spectacle. Don't forget to come out of the premise and gorge on the lovely puchka stalls situated bang opposite to the main gate.

20. A Day in the Museum

Ninth oldest in the world. Largest in India. Magnificently built structure. Gigantic courtyard. Once upon a time called 'Jadhughar' or House of Magic. Some of the world's most mysterious fossils, paintings, murals, sculptures, gemstones and paintings nestled in one compound. Regular workshops. Excellently organized. Regular book readings. An Egyptian mummy which retains its heart despite all other organs being extracted from it. The Indian Museum is one of the most exciting compounds that I used to be a regular at, given my incredible love for history. You must pay it a visit just for its incredible library.

Anisha Mandal

>TOURIST

"The pure, the bright, the beautiful, That stirred our hearts in youth, The impulse to a wordless prayer, The dreams of love and truth; The longings after something lost, The spirit's yearning cry, The striving after better hopes ... These things can never die."

- Ruskin Bond, Night Train to Deoli and Other Stories

Anisha Mandal

21. Forever Young at 250: The Great Banyan Tree

Not many Banyan Trees in the world have Wikipedia pages dedicated to them. Nobody has a historical account of planting this tree but ever since I read about it, it has been 250 years old. It must be, if so goes the historical lore. Quaint yet sturdy, it stands in all its glory in the Acharya Jagadish Chandra Bose Botanical Gardens. The Botanical Gardens with all its exotic blooms is in itself a great place to visit and feel close to the greens in the middle of urbanity, but sitting under this tree has a charm of its own. It'll make you feel like picking up an Oscar Wilde short story, or a few verses from Hemingway, just to feel that everything in the world must really be alright.

22. A Novice's Guide to Shopping for the Right Saree

The famed Indian nine yards, designed to visually represent femininity in its most gorgeous fashion has come a long, long way in terms of fabric, design, print, style of draping and idea. Bengal contributes to the history of the saree in very significant ways. In fact, the tradition of making and selling sarees is hereditary- there are famed families known just for this. While pop cult has deified the 'Laal Paar Shada Shaari' or Red-bordered white saree as the Bangali saree, there are a hundred different kinds of textiles made in Bengal that are spun into their saree stitches and handed over to the extremely skilled for working on the print or stitch work on them. The best cotton sarees come from Bengal and the Handwork sarees are bound to make your heart skip a beat. Kohl-line your eyes, pick up a pair of silver or bronze earrings, wear a Bindi (traditionally a red dot worn on the centre of the forehead), get that perfectly-fitted blouse stitched to accentuate your curves, pick up a petticoat that hugs your waist just right and you're all set to adorn a saree of your choice. I will enlist some of my favourite kinds of sarees but not even the most detailed explanations of what they are like will be able to do justice to physically holding them and really understanding the fabric. Sarees are sentimental pieces of clothing. My grandmother still has all the sarees that her parents had gifted her for all her birthdays, but saree stories make for a separate, elaborate, irrelevant discussion.

- **The Taant Saree-** A product of the best minds of the handloom industry in Bengal.
- **The Tussar Silk Saree-** Understated colours, woefully expensive, but a fabric so gorgeous with the patterns of its spinning process clearly visible, I could die in one of these with a grin on my face.
- **The Murshidabad Silk Saree-** A rare kind of silk, I associate this saree with unadulterated nostalgia.
- **The Jamdani Saree-** This one's an ornate kind meant specially for the big occasions of life. Partially sheer, it

often comes with a golden border work.

- **The Knatha Stitch Saree -** A collector's heart could roll through the length of this intricately hand done thread work saree.

- **The Baatik Print Saree-** Think tie-and-dye and imagine it done specifically for the whole of the nine yards. This is for the woman who'd like to look not-so-festive on an ordinary day or not-so-ordinary on a festive day.

- **The Tangail Silk Saree-** The lustre, the shine, the finish, the colours- it is everything regal, everything bold. A lady in a red Tangail saree looks her gorgeous best, in my opinion.

- **The Khesh Saree-** You can wear these to work when you feel happy- They are light, incredible soft, drape around you like a dream and very inexpensive. There's something so fuss-free about this airy, breathable saree, that the urban-modern girl seems to have her edginess heightened by the feel of it.

>TOURIST

I am leaving you with the names of my grandmother's favourite saree shops, hoping that it gives you good direction-
The Indian Silk House, Adi Dhakeshwari Bastralaya, Kanishka's, Gourisaria, Ananda.

23. Dhoti Secrets: The Fashionista in the Bengali Man

Every time I visualize Byomkesh Bakshy, this incredibly sexy Bengali detective from our pages of fiction, my heart skips random beats. It's got to be that dhoti. In all these years of observing them, I have only noticed how the modern Bengali Man, at least most of them, shy away from the idea of wearing a Dhoti. An unstitched 5 metre cloth that is draped around the waist and legs and knotted at the waist, the Dhoti is available in a variety of fabrics and is a part of the South Indian, Nepalese and Bengali traditional clothing legacy. But give the man an airy Kurta-Pajama, a longish, collarless shirt of sorts with a baggy trouser of sorts, and he often looks his disarming best.

The Bangalis call the Kurta, Panjabi. This Panjabi when paired with the Dhoti is what men traditionally get married in. It's all sorts of coy and charming, in stark contrast to what the modern man thinks of it. Though there is a wide array of fabrics that lend it its versatility, the white-cotton-panjabi-and-dhoti combination has a simpering impact. Given that it comes with the modest, confident smile of the Bengali man in between great conversation, it's quite a visual treat.

I would highly recommend going to the South Kolkata shopping complex, Dakshinapan, as your one stop shopping destination for all things ethnic. If not, there's a corner in South Kolkata's Gariahat Road with a vast array of shops catering to the needs of the Bengali Man's fashion needs, my favourite shop being Panjabi-Stores. As a child, I too would wear the Panjabi-Pajama during the winters. I would always be bowled over by the way all the men in the store knew the exact sizes and fabrics and prints and where they were kept in their loft. Just watching them display the options to you is a treat in itself.

If you're a handloom person, make a trip to the Khadi Bhawan or Fab India. Don't forget to get yourself the traditional golden or ivory buttons for the Panjabi.

24. The Ghats- A City Outlined by the Ganges

India flourishes as a civilization because of the might river Ganga or Ganges that flows through its length and breadth. When the Ganges comes to Bengal, it is then called the Hooghly River. Kolkata is a linear city along the banks of the Ganges. A Ghat is mostly a flight of steps that leads to the river, except that it is much more than that. A Ghat is the birthplace of livelihood, the breathing ground of religion and occupation, and solace to an artist's poignant heart. These Ghats also observe the performance of the last rites for the Hindus. The Baboo Ghat is one such ghat which is always bustling with barbers and masseurs and boatmen.

The Princep Ghat is my favourite ghat, witness to many a romantic or morose evening. You must avail one of the boat rides at the Princep Ghat. The boatmen often sing folks songs, and you'll watch other bigger boats with fishermen preparing their meal. A sunset at Princep Ghat will leave you with your much needed respite.

25. We're a Fishy Lot

Before you picked up this book, you must have already known that us Bengalis eat, love, glorify and eulogize our fish. An easy forty odd types of mostly freshwater fish wiggle their ways into our markets and our kitchens in innumerable kilos every day. There are more than a few hundred different ways in which we cook our fish, across cuisines. In the traditional Bangali cuisine itself there would be an easy hundred different fish recipes. Each variety has at least 50 odd traditional recipes associated with them and this permutation combination of recipes and varieties is endless. Maybe one day a Bengali mathematician will take it upon herself or himself to decode the love for fish in numbers. You cannot not go to our slightly smelly fish markets and observe a first hand experience of what the madness is all about, especially on Sunday mornings. The queen of all fish is of course, the Hilsa or Ilish, as we call it.

If you're in Kolkata, you must try the Rui, the Bhetki, the Chingri or Prawns, the Katla, the Pomfret, the Tangra, the Pabda, the

Parshe, the Shole, the Magur, the Tilapia, the Koi, the Topshe, I don't see this list ending any time soon. Just go strike up a conversation with any Bengali about fish. Of course, some Bengalis aren't the biggest fans, but that lot is an easy minority. I tend to look at them with polite nods and sympathetic eyes. You cannot come to Kolkata and not make a meal out of the legendary Fish Fry or the Bhetki Paturi or the Chingri Machh'er Malaicurry or the Shorshe Ilish. Take a piece of paper and pen, and copy down these names and just hand it over to anybody on the streets of Kolkata. They'll point towards a direction that will help you meet your lip smacking destination.

26. As Grave as it Gets

The ancient premises of a mosque, the unkempt backyards of churches, so many Muslim burial grounds, that one unsung Jewish burial ground, not to forget the large expanse that the Chinese have allotted to pay homage to the departed, Kolkata's "underground" world is as cosmopolitan as the visible world. If you're a connoisseur of spine chilling moments or someone who is fascinated by the history epitaphs bear, you might want to visit each of these cemeteries. The Park Street cemetery is probably the most well known of all and is home to Henry Vivian Derozio's grave. But the lesser known, not so talked about graveyards often have epitaphs with the richest lines known to mankind. There are tourist agencies in Kolkata who these days take people on haunted-place-walks and often take them to graveyards, but I'm not a fan of the silly-ness that transpires in these events. I'd rather advocate stopping by a grave and wondering about life as the person might have known it to be.

27. India's First Organ Sits Shy Here: St.John's Cathedral

The year was 1784. The man laying the foundation stone was Warren Hastings. A tiny museum still carries his legendary desk and chair. An underrated beauty in Neoclassical architectural style. Almost always empty.

There's a wonderful man, who is now significantly old with a hip injury, who still comes down to pursue his musical career in Gospel, who goes by the name Johnny Purty who you absolutely have to meet when you're paying a visit to Kolkata. He's almost always up for a long chat. He also prides himself in being one of the first musicians in the city. When the first organ in India was installed in the compound, he was only a little boy. With time, the instrument became his learning ground, and I have goose bumps while I write this. Situated right behind the Governor's House with a vast and gorgeous compound, keep this as one of the first places that you would want to visit.

28. Vociferous Debating- Ends with Songs and Hugs

The Calcutta Debating Society is of course privy to all sorts of the many intellectual discourses that Kolkata thrives on for belief, living and I'd daresay, entertainment, but the best debates happen impromptu in Kolkata, in random discussion forums. Drop by a film screening at SRFTI, or a night of spoken word at The Doodle Room, or a seminar at Jadavpur University, or a talk at Presidency University, or the everyday steps of Dakshinapan.

What you have to remember during these sessions is to be a good, good listener. Everybody eventually goes home happy and being a rationalist, but a keen ear during these sessions shed light on some of the deepest insights about life. Of course, this might be true for most cities in the world but most cities in the world don't have the bone of a passionate debater like the Bangali.

29. Night Crawlers, Ahoy!

Contrary to popular belief, Kolkata has an amazing night life. If you're a pub person, there are innumerable places to stop by and glug. If you want to dance your bare heels off, there are some very exciting places for you to drop by.

The Park Hotel remains my absolute favourite. Despite newer places opening up every now and then, there's something about that complex that keeps taking us back there for the night when you want to unwind with your friends and meet a lot of amiable strangers. Tantra and Roxy are two places for those who like their music loud and can't wait to flaunt their dance moves. The ladies always have an added advantage in Kolkata- every day of the week there's a Ladies Night in some place or the other. While the drinks are free, one must be careful not to be left with an awful hangover that ruins the first half of the second day on vacation. For some great food post the midnight hour, there's always Sharma Dhaba or Jai Hind Dhaba, that cook up storms for the hunger pangs.

30. The Race Course- Just like Old Times!

Established in 1820 and maintained by the Royal Calcutta Turf Club, the Kolkata Race Course hosts races all through the year on Saturdays and public holidays, except December, January, February and October.

Fashion is just another name for the madness that you witness during these races. People still betting, the grandest of horses on display from all parts of the world, ladies and gentlemen dressed like the British never really left the country at all, it is a sight to behold. I've never had much of a taste for the carnival of style and flamboyance that transpires during these races, but it's a good lesson in human psychology and history and for pretty much anybody who would want a taste of Pre-Partition days. It's pretty exclusive as an event but Kolkata's top-notch hospitality is always open to tourists being a part of these cultural extravaganzas.

Anisha Mandal

"The most beautiful things in the world cannot be seen or touched, they are felt with the heart."

- Antoine de Saint-Exupery, The Little Prince

Anisha Mandal

31. The Wedding Reds, Whites and Golds

A traditional Bengali Hindu wedding is all about the fanciful kaleidoscope with heightened reds, whites and golds, wherever you look, with the extravagant Bengali meals wafting through the air and disappearing into hungry mouths in between loud conversations and the sound of the Shehnai playing.

The brides are a spectacle in the red, benarasi saree, the groom is a nervous bloke in a traditional, ivory, slightly funny, hat or the topor, and countless relatives complimenting each other dressed at their traditional, gorgeous best, all trying to make the big day, a little more special in their own ways. One can write a whole book on a Bengali wedding, but to behold the sight of one is a must-do in Bengal. What's better? The ceremonies last for four days, mostly. If you know of a Bengali, or you look somebody up on the internet, or throw in a request in the internet universe and find a couple about to get married, they'll be more than happy to have you over on their most bluesy days.

32. The Political Artery

Crash Course- There is a very visible, perpetually throbbing artery in every person in Kolkata which makes half of them powerhouses of robust knowledge and understanding of human behaviour or just indignant dolts. Either way, if you're in Kolkata, come prepared to understand the political landscape of Bengal and the country in short lessons that almost every conversation will furnish you with. Most importantly, learn about the Naxalite movement and the 1971 Bangladesh Liberation War. Observe the stains of pathos that both left on the walls of Kolkata. There is a lane in North Kolkata known as the Naxal lane. The headquarters of the two leading political parties of Kolkata make for excellent visits- Alimuddin Street which is a Communist party of India Marxist locality and Kalighat which is a Trinamool Congress locality. Trinamool Congress is the reigning political party and was a much needed break from the 34 years of farcical communist asphyxiation in Kolkata but both parties have been regular disappointments, any which way, as is the case in democracies all across the world. The

Bharatiya Janata Party is slowly trying to seep into the political spectrum in a ridiculous bright orange, but they have a long way to go before they become significant regionally. Dig up facts, do your research, have Kolkata help you shape opinions and above all, have faith in the masses and pursue these extremely enlightening discussions.

33. Biryani. Period.

We are home to the best Biryani in the world, and if anybody wants to contest that, I am willing to invest a lifetime of debating until I, deservingly, prove myself right. Though, over a plate of Biryani, please. Aromatic, spiced rice, with luscious chicken or mutton pieces, the most enchanting combination of flavours, that piece of boiled potato that people can have wars over, and a naïve boiled egg. Served piping hot. Traditionally from Lucknow, but by way of political conquests and God's grace travelled to our city, the great Kolkata Biryani single-handedly rules the hearts of all those who have tasted it. Like most dishes, it has its variations, but no matter where you have it, it is still a work of hypnotism. My personal favourite biryani places are- Zum zum, Zeeshan, Arsalan, Royal Indian Hotel, Asma and Aminia. We often joke that when the country sees the peak of communal tension between Hindus and Muslims, the Kolkata Biryani will be the only route to a peaceful resolution.

34. A Filmlover's Muse

The heartland of the greatest filmmakers of the country, Satyajit Ray, Ritwik Ghatak and Mrinal Sen, Kolkata boasts its love for films unabashedly. It is safe to say that every locality is home to a filmmaker, countless film lovers and many a self proclaimed film critic. The centre point of one of the biggest film industries of the country- Tollywood, Kolkata loves films from across the world. The Kolkata Film Festival is the second oldest film International film festival of the country, held from the 10th to the 17th of November every year. One of the best film-institutes of Asia is the Satyajit Ray Film and Television Institute, right here. You might want to drop by.

35. The Inviting Campus Culture- Jadavpur University

The only University of its kind in the eastern part of India where just about anybody is welcome to come embrace the culture, even if it's just as a visitor. Graffiti walls, always a buzzing fervor of poetry and politics, a breeding ground for live music, lots of dogs who call it home, professors who would invite you for conversation whenever you want to pop questions, students who will gleefully show you around, little lakes that you can sit by, seven canteens that could put restaurants to shame, the Jadavpur University campus is a must visit. I'm a proud alma mater but my words are testified by the oddest of strangers from the oddest corners of the world. Here's a line from a song about this Kolkata 32 campus that makes my eyes well up-

"Tomar bidesh jurey naam, Kolkata'r obhimaan"

"You are famed across the world, Kolkata's pride"

36. Checkmate Under a Flyover

It is legitimate- there is a ledge of sorts under the Gariahat flyover where religiously, at all hours in the day, but especially in the evening, people stop by to simply play Chess.

You might have realized by now that Kolkata is all about intellectual gratification and continuously looking at honing their brain, so this is not supposed to be entirely surprising. Except that it was, when it suddenly started one fine day.

Street chess, unbothered by the weather, traffic or anything else.

The Kolkata Chess Club has some hundred odd members, I think, but passers by interested in a good game, or simply want to watch these maestros of the checkerboard from all sorts of occupations and age groups are more than just welcome.

We are cool like that.

37. The Infectious Energy of Local Markets

I fleetingly mentioned the fish markets while letting you know about what transpires in the fish business. Here is a more detailed account. The average local market is bustling with energy at all hours. A spectacle in colour and glory and stench and all sorts of stalls and shops, other than lost love there's nothing that you cannot find in these big complexes. If you're lucky, that too, perhaps.

Grocery stores, local departmental stores, all sorts of fruits and vegetables, every imaginable edible, stationery shops, little nurseries, toy stores, hardware stores, name it and you have it. Two of my favourite local markets would be the Gariahat Market and the Lake Market. I must warn you in advance that visiting markets during the 2.30 p.m to 4 p.m window is futile. Bengalis are famous for the siesta culture.

38. New Market- Some Things Never Go Out of Vogue

Chaotic, yes. Sometimes suffocating, yes. But all the public roads and tiny stand alone shopping complexes coming together to create this old school vibe for shoppers and stoppers alike- everything is forgiven for New Market. It is the city's oldest shopping destination and the most sought after in the eastern part of the country, back in the day. The latest trends always hit this road first. It dates back to 1874 and still attracts an easy 2 to 3 odd thousand visitors every weekend evening. Keep your bargaining skills handy and the number of things that you will be able to purchase in under INR 5,000 is unimaginable. Sunglasses for INR 100 that last for years, anybody?

Also, a part of the market is reserved for all kinds of meat and makes for a meat-lover's paradise.

You cannot not be in Kolkata and not go to New Market.

39. A Clayman's Breathing Ground

The traditional Bengali Potter is no less a magician. I intend my puns. Kumortoli in North Kolkata is the breeding, breathing ground for these extremely talented clay artisans whose best works come to life during the October festive season. These potters used to be patronized by the rich, elite families who were passionate about tradition and had the money and fancy for clay works. But after the disintegration of many of these families, a lot of these potters have vanished. A struggler's life with a hereditary craft in a world struggling to maintain the fine balance between practical goods and fanciful art pieces, Kumortoli is your escape from reality. Do drop by and request a chance to touch a potter's wheel here in this part of the world, once. It really is an honour.

40. Suruchi Restaurant- By women who don't need justification since 1969

Dejected by society, affected by the Partition, with nowhere to go, with no respite to be found, a bunch of women came together to start a canteen in 1969, taking it upon themselves to master the culinary arts. Today, it's a full fledged restaurant that runs full-house during lunch owing to their lip smacking dishes in traditional Bengali cuisine.

Normally, people harp about the College Street Coffee House being a must visit, which it really is with its trunk full of history, but I've always believed in taking people to Suruchi and it has always been a time-proven hit.

There's nothing on the menu at this Elliot Road restaurant that won't work wonders for you.

Give this a shot. Without fail.

Anisha Mandal

"And the air was full of Thoughts and Things to Say. But at times like these, only the Small Things are ever said. Big Things lurk unsaid inside."

— Arundhati Roy,

The God of Small Things

Anisha Mandal

41. 130 Year Old Flower Market

Countless garlands of flowers coiled around each other and around their owners like a festivity of colourful anacondas as Mullick Ghat, a vast expanse that smells hypnotic at all times, this 130 year old flower market is not a very easily frequented place, though it should be.

All imaginable colours come alive as the soundscape of the place is like a rhythmic buzz, with scores and scores of flower vendors are lined everyday with the backdrop of the great Howrah Bridge. Vigour and exuberance find a new meaning in this market hailed as one of Asia's largest flower markets.

You'll have to be an early riser to watch it at its best, the vendors start the day as early as 5.00 a.m.

42. You're Never Too Old for Music- Instruments from Bengal

As of last week, the sitar George Harrison used in the recording of the song 'Norwegian Wood' was sold at $62,500.

The sitar was made in an old shop for musical instruments from the by-lanes of Kolkata.It , apparently, had changed his life. It is not surprising to know that the oldest musical instrument shops of Kolkata really were witness to the highs and lows of many musicians from across the world.A very significant part of the vibrant diversity that Bengal is all about are two extremely culturally inclined and musically talented communities. One would be the Santals. The other would be the Bauls. There are many a musical instrument attributed to both these communities. Most significantly, a bamboo flute or 'Tiriao' and a cylindrical drum or 'madal' accompanies the traditional Jhumur song-and-dance practices of the Santals who are among the earliest natives of the subcontinent.

The tradition of the Bauls or the spiritual bohemians whose

fascinating culture, music and lifestyle has inspired the greatest writers and spiritual seekers is centered around their music. Always accompanied by an Ektara or a Single-string instrument, or a Dotara, a double-string instrument, or a Khamak, another single string instrument, their music is raw and in the praise of the ultimate truth of the Universe. The instruments might be inexpensive and fairly easy to play, but having the right sound that exemplifies a Baul's love or woe takes a lifetime's worth of practice.

All these instruments are easily available in the old streets of Kolkata- you just have to ask somebody for direction.

While we're on the subject, you might also want to pay a visit to the Baul Fakir Utsav that happens every winter in Kolkata and witnesses a conglomerate of Bauls from all across the land and beyond in a carnival-esque environment.

43. Birla Mandir- Years of Hardwork

Ideated and built by the industrialist family, the Birlas, this gorgeous monumental structure embodies magnificence in its marble bears.

It took 26 whole years for building this temple, bit by bit, a process that a lot of living residents of Kolkata have witnessed unfold before their eyes in 1996.

Of all the temples in Kolkata, I'd pick this to let you know about because of the moments of peace that you are enveloped in while sitting in the premises of the temple, simply because of the silence it fills you with, despite being situated on a very busy road in South Kolkata.

What makes it all the more special is the fact that below it lies the G.D Birla Sabhaghar Auditorium, which is one of my favourite auditoriums in the country that has hosted some of the biggest names in theatre from across the country. Watch a play, if you may.

44. Nakhoda Masjid- Leftovers of Akbar's Influence

The busiest street of Kolkata, Burrabazaar, is home to this piece of absolute wonder. The Nakhoda Masjid is one of my favourite spots in Kolkata, especially on the days when one would like to take the camera out on a date. Emperor Akbar's mausoleum in Agra inspired the construction of this picturesque mosque with its three domes and two minarets, stained glass windows, a prayer space that accommodates 10,000 odd people, and simply the smell of rust, prayer, old books, and handmade perfumes which amalgamate in the air and drift into your nostrils to charm you. The ablution pool looks like a mystery that will never reveal itself. The name Nakhoda means Mariner, which just makes in infinitely more romantic.

The huge granite gate cannot wait to welcome you.

45. Romancing by the Lake

Bengali couples, throughout time, have learned to romance by the lake.

The most famous destination for romance in South Kolkata thus, has been the Dhakuria Lake. A space for the old and the fitness enthusiasts to avail, it often seems that the expanse rightfully really belongs only to the couples. Nestled in the corners of benches, or right by the Lake, they are too busy whispering sweet nothings into each other's ears.

But just on its own, the Lake is a very romantic spot in the evenings, especially in the winters.

A cup of hot lemon tea served to you by tea sellers, and a few nuts to munch on, and you can stare into the little expanse of water and enjoy some quiet time by yourself.

46. Saltlake, Rajarhat: Kolkata Spreads Wings

Saltlake was all unkempt forest like as a locality and Rajarhat was all about fisheries. Until Kolkata spread its wings to embrace both into being a part of its history and legacy.

Well planned, modern, broad roads, extremely confusing, clean, less polluted streets, and a lot of quiet in stark contrast to the rest of Kolkata, these two places have now been lined with large entertainment hubs and enterprises by some of the biggest names of the hospitality industry in the country.

The one place that I would strongly recommend to you would be the Eco Park. Fairly new, this huge ecological park is usually a weekend getaway spot for the people in the city. A 480 acres plot with a 104 acres water body in between and a little island, it has a bamboo garden, a bonsai garden, a butterfly garden, urban recreational spaces, other themed gardens, ecological zones like wetlands, grasslands and urban forests. It also has a tiny eco-resort. You might fancy a trip.

47. The Tramconductor's Ting-ting-ting

"Chol rastay shaji tramline" - Come lets lay down tramlines on the road. 125 operational trams that people avail for regular transportation and over 25 tramlines, Kolkata is the only city in the country where trams are still functional, and one of the few in the world at that. The oldest electric trams in Asia, set up in 1902, it has come a along way from being a horse-drawn system to the current A.C ones which also offer heritage tram rides these days. Hop on to one when you spot it, or go pay a visit to the Gariahat Tram Depot and go where it takes you for a unique tour of Kolkata.

While you can pre-book a heritage tram ride that comes complete with a tourist guide, I'd strongly recommend you to do it on your own. The A.C tram rides, in all honesty, are no fun at all. The wooden paneling inside, the chrome of the light, the conductor in his atypical attire, a tram ride is a vision in sepia.

48. Oil Lamps and Chanting by the Ganges- Belur Math

Forty acres sounding of chanting, lit brass oil lamps all across the western ghats of the Hooghly, you don't need to be religious at all to seek solace in the evenings at the Belur Math, a monastery where Sri Ramakrishna spent the last phase of his life.

In his words- "The blazing light of universal harmony that will emanate from here will flood the whole world."

A serene campus, lush green lawns, and the luxury of dipping your feet in the Hooghly and staring out at the distant horizon with the water full of reflections of the blazing lamps.

You cannot not come here.

49. Marble Palace- 19th Century Elegance

46, Muktaram Babu Street was bestowed by the splendor and impressiveness of this palatial mansion of North Kolkata, a subject of reverie in white.

Built in 1835 by Raja Rajendra Mullick, the house is still a residence to his descendents. The Neoclassical architectural style is Kolkata's darling influence for gorgeous mansions. Interestingly, the first zoo that ever opened in India is the Marble Palace Zoo, situated right beside the mansion. Though now, it is only an aviary. While the entry is fee, photography is prohibited. To walk around this vision, you must obtain a permit 24 hours in advance from the West Bengal Tourism Information Bureau situated at B.B.D Bag Kolkata. It's open 10 a.m to 4 p.m on almost all days except Thursdays.

50. The Kolkata Soundscape

Every road , every street corner has its own distinct sound, like any other city in the world. But there's just something about Kolkata's soundscape. From Victoria Memorial to North Kolkata, from Gariahat Market to Park Street, from the by lanes of Ballygunge, to the stillness of Salt Lake, stop in the city sometimes and just listen to the city hum all the time.

Words in Bangla, phrases of endearment, some loud profanities, odd traces of music everywhere you go, so many dreams being whispered at all times, so many dreams are let gone of at all times, the most emotional airport of the country, the railway tracks which are privy to the unfairness of Kolkata's economy, hear it all, embrace it all, and keep it in your heart. You will end up visiting the Calcutta High Court, the Shahid Minar, Fluryys, Au Bon Pain, Oly Pub, the Coffee House and so many more places that are the regular spots of attraction but I haven't elaborated on them. When you go to any of these places or the ones that I've listed, just stop and shut your eyes and listen to the old ischemic heartbeat of Kolkata that skips when it falls in love, that pauses when its children leave for bigger cities and dreams, that cry at every homecoming, all the time.

And when you've really heard Kolkata, you'll have heard the most beautiful song any city has ever sung to your aching heart.

>TOURIST

Top Reasons to Book This Trip

- **Food**. Nobody does it better in India.

- **The people**. Hailed as 'sweetest' for a reason.

- **Fervor and festivity**. We really know how to celebrate.

- **History**. We wear like old wood or white musk perfume.

- **Books and Poets**.

- **Music**. Performances that will leave you gaping in awe.

- **The old tram**.

- **Romance**.

Anisha Mandal

> TOURIST

GREATER THAN A TOURIST

Visit GreaterThanATourist.com
http://GreaterThanATourist.com

Sign up for the Greater Than a Tourist Newsletter
http://eepurl.com/cxspyf

Follow us on Facebook:
https://www.facebook.com/GreaterThanATourist

Follow us on Pinterest:
http://pinterest.com/GreaterThanATourist

Follow us on Instagram:
http://Instagram.com/GreaterThanATourist

Anisha Mandal

GREATER THAN A TOURIST

Please leave your honest review of this book on Amazon and Goodreads. Thank you.

We appreciate your positive and negative feedback as we try to provide tourist guidance in their next trip from a local.

Our Story

Traveling is a passion of the "Greater than a Tourist" series creator. Lisa studied abroad in college, and for their honeymoon Lisa and her husband toured Europe. During her travels to Malta, an older man tried to give her some advice based on his own experience living on the island since he was a young boy. She was not sure if she should talk to the stranger but was interested in his advice. When traveling to some places she was wary to talk to locals because she was afraid that they weren't being genuine. Through her travels, Lisa learned how much locals had to share with tourists. Lisa created the "Greater Than a Tourist" book series to help connect people with locals. A topic that locals are very passionate about sharing.

Anisha Mandal

Notes

Made in the USA
Columbia, SC
23 July 2018